CONCERT FAVORITES

Volume 2

Band Arrangements Correlated with Essential Elements Band Method Book

ISBN 978-1-4234-0088-2

HAL•LEONARD®

7777 W. BLUEMOUND RD. P.O. BOX 13819 MILWAUKEE, WI 53213

00860176

BANDROOM BOOGIE

PERCUSSION 1
Snare Drum, Bass Drum

MICHAEL SWEENEY

00860176

BANDROOM BOOGIE

3

PERCUSSION 2
Sus. Cym.

MICHAEL SWEENEY

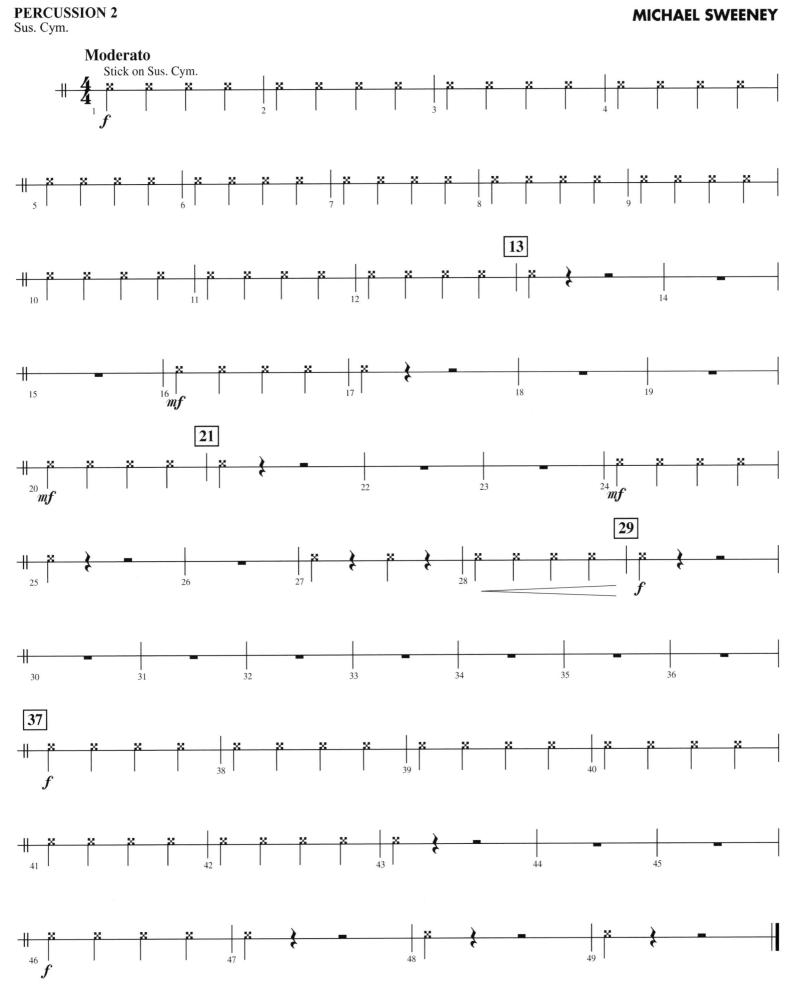

00860176

BEETHOVEN'S NINTH

PERCUSSION
(S.D., B.D.)

LUDWIG VAN BEETHOVEN
Arranged by PAUL LAVENDER

00860176

ROYAL FIREWORKS MUSIC

5

GEORGE FREDERIC HANDEL
Arranged by MICHAEL SWEENEY

TIMPANI

00860176

GALLANT MARCH

PERCUSSION 1
Snare Drum, Bass Drum

MICHAEL SWEENEY

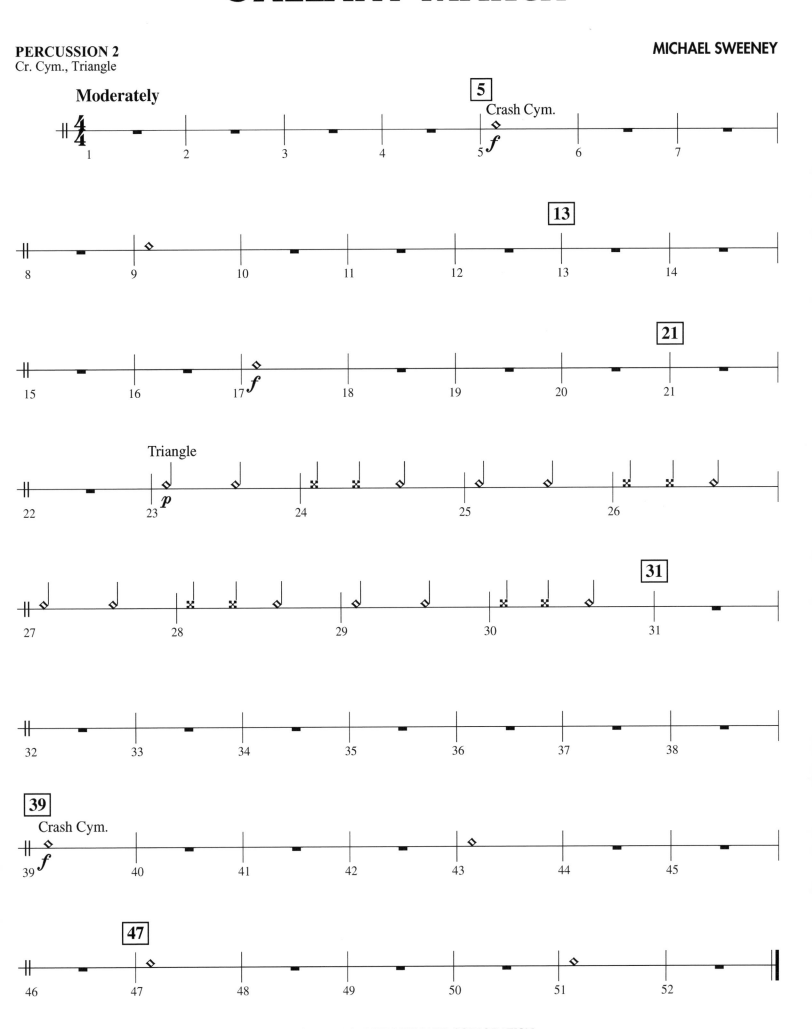

GALLANT MARCH

PERCUSSION 2
Cr. Cym., Triangle

MICHAEL SWEENEY

HIGH ADVENTURE

PERCUSSION 1
Snare Drum, Bass Drum

PAUL LAVENDER

HIGH ADVENTURE

PERCUSSION 2
Cr. Cym., Triangle

PAUL LAVENDER

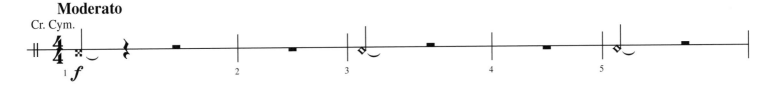

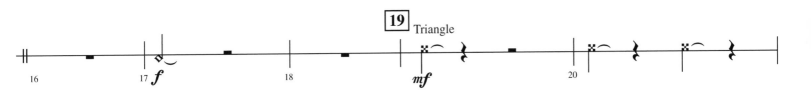

00860176

ROCK & ROLL - PART II
(The Hey Song)

PERCUSSION 1
Snare Drum, Bass Drum

Words and Music by
MIKE LEANDER and **GARY GLITTER**
Arranged by PAUL LAVENDER

00860176

ROCK & ROLL - PART II
(The Hey Song)

PERCUSSION 2
Sus. Cym., Tamb.

Words and Music by
MIKE LEANDER and **GARY GLITTER**
Arranged by PAUL LAVENDER

Steady Rock

Sus. Cym.
(w/ stick)

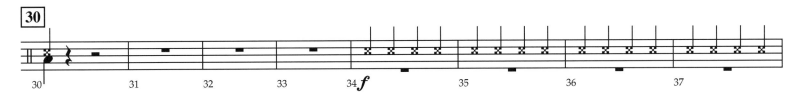

00860176

AMAZING GRACE

PERCUSSION 1
Snare Drum, Bass Drum

Traditional American Melody
Arranged by PAUL LAVENDER

AMAZING GRACE

Traditional American Melody
Arranged by PAUL LAVENDER

PERCUSSION 2
Cr. Cym., Sus. Cym.

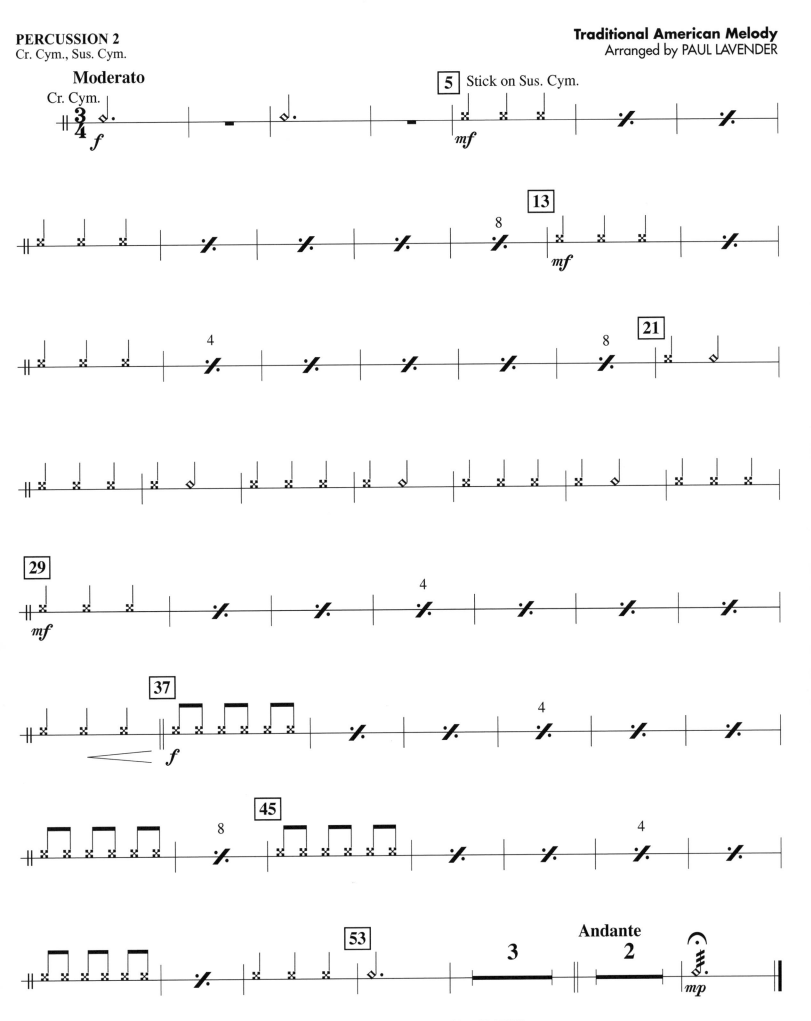

PERCUSSION 1
(S.D., B.D.)

INFINITY
(Concert March)

JAMES CURNOW (ASCAP)

00860176

PERCUSSION 2
(Cr. Cym.)

INFINITY
(Concert March)

JAMES CURNOW (ASCAP)

Moderately Fast

Cr. Cym.

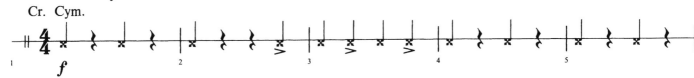
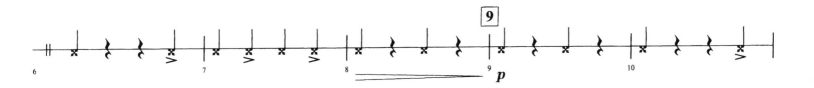

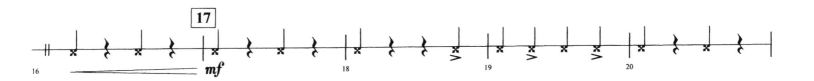
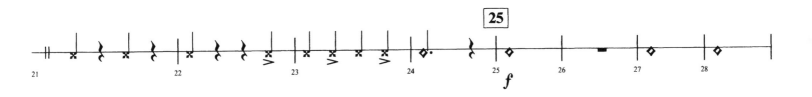
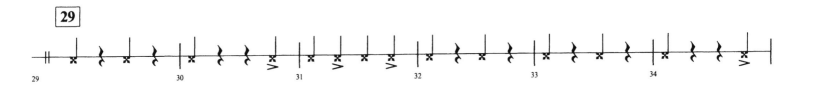
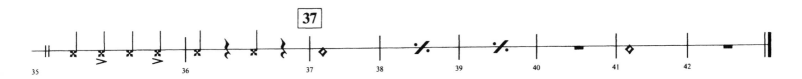

00860176

LATIN FIRE

PERCUSSION 1
Snare Drum, Bass Drum

JOHN HIGGINS

LATIN FIRE

PERCUSSION 2
Sus. Cym., Maracas (or Shaker)

JOHN HIGGINS

LINUS AND LUCY

PERCUSSION 1
Snare Drum, Bass Drum

By VINCE GUARALDI
Arranged by MICHAEL SWEENEY

LINUS AND LUCY

PERCUSSION 2
Sus. Cym.

By VINCE GUARALDI
Arranged by MICHAEL SWEENEY

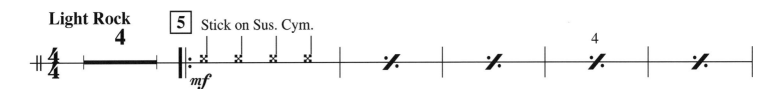

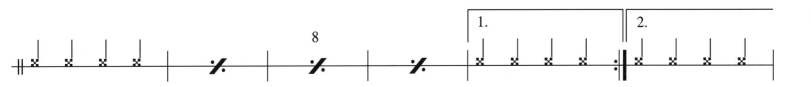

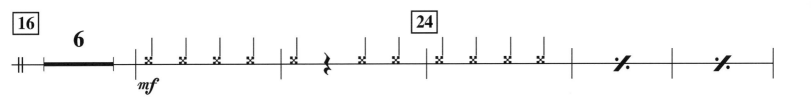

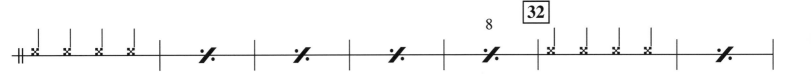

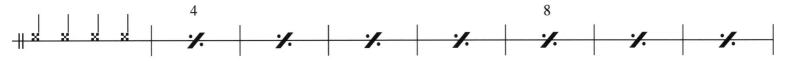

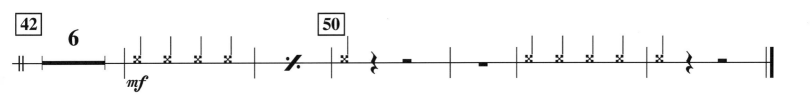

(From The Paramount Motion Picture STAR TREK GENERATIONS)

THEME FROM "STAR TREK® GENERATIONS"

PERCUSSION 1
(S.D., B.D.)

Music by DENNIS McCARTHY
Arranged by MICHAEL SWEENEY

00860176

THEME FROM "STAR TREK® GENERATIONS"

PERCUSSION 2
(Cr. Cym., Sus. Cym.)

Music by DENNIS McCARTHY
Arranged by MICHAEL SWEENEY

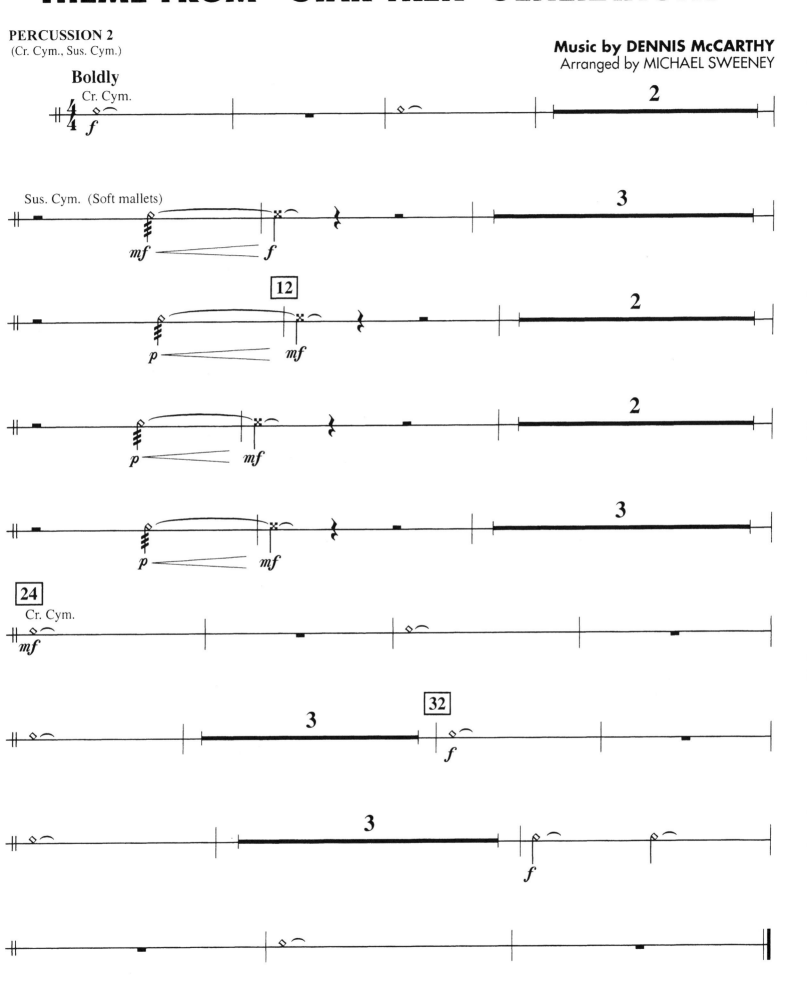

AMERICAN SPIRIT MARCH

PERCUSSION 1
Snare Drum, Bass Drum

JOHN HIGGINS

AMERICAN SPIRIT MARCH

PERCUSSION 2
Cr. Cym., Wood Block

JOHN HIGGINS

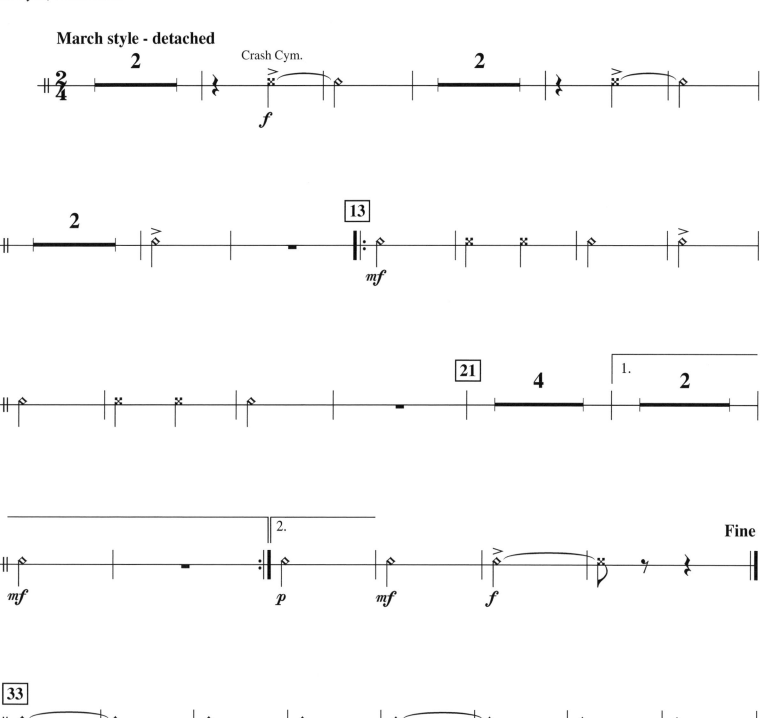

00860176

GATHERING IN THE GLEN

PERCUSSION 1
Snare Drum, Bass Drum

MICHAEL SWEENEY

GATHERING IN THE GLEN

PERCUSSION 2
Triangle, Cr. Cym., Sus. Cym.

MICHAEL SWEENEY

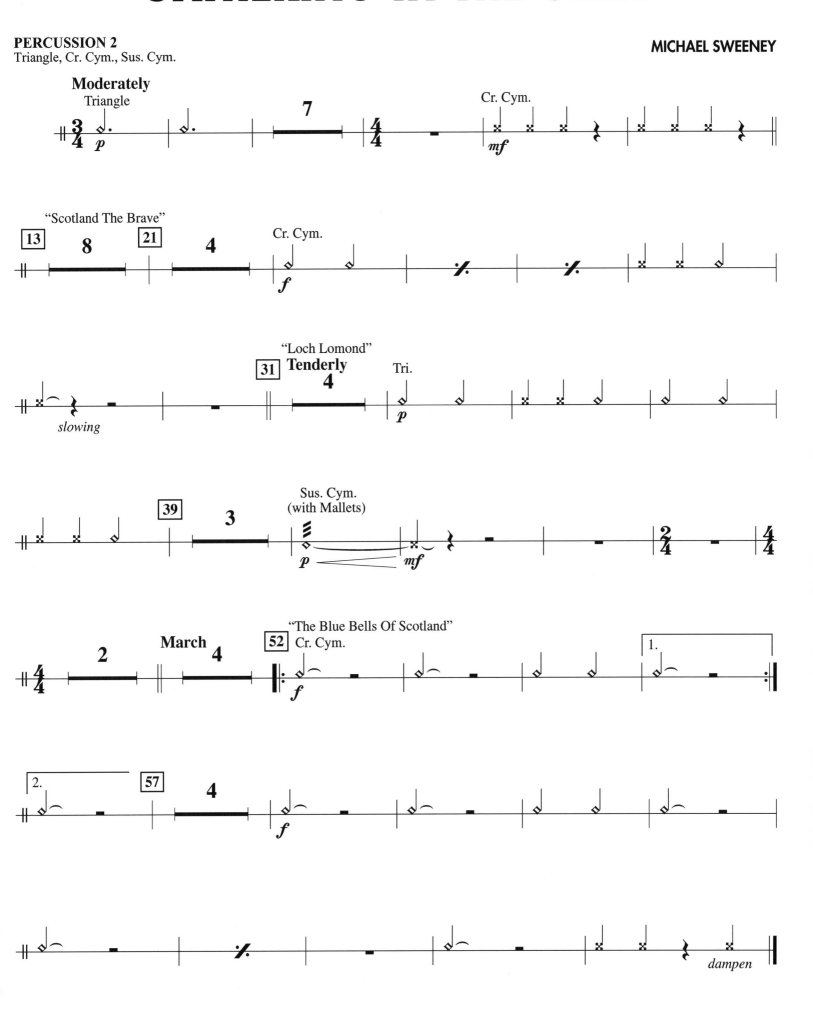

THE LOCO-MOTION

PERCUSSION 1
S.D., B.D.

Words and Music by
GERRY GOFFIN and CAROLE KING
Arranged by JOHN HIGGINS

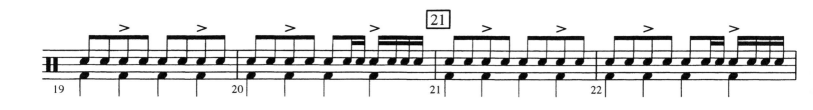

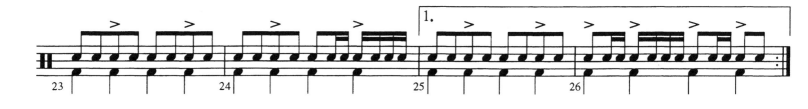

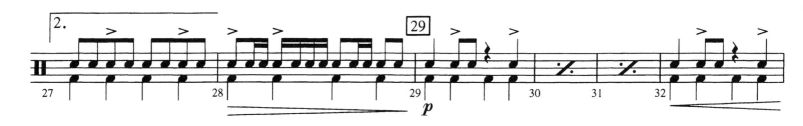

00860176

THE LOCO-MOTION

PERCUSSION 2
Sus. Cym., Tamb.

**Words and Music by
GERRY GOFFIN and CAROLE KING**
Arranged by JOHN HIGGINS

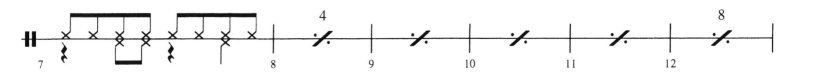

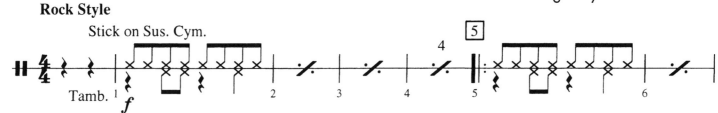

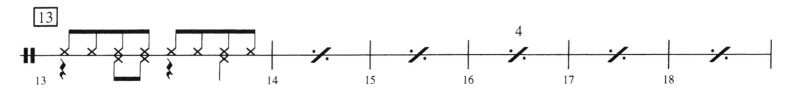

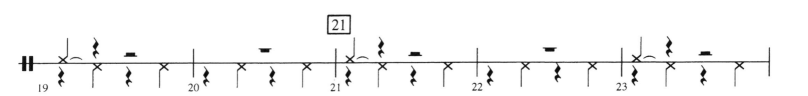

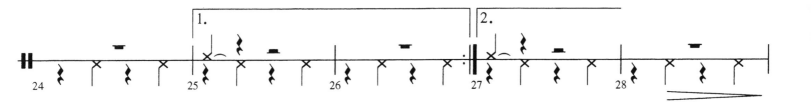

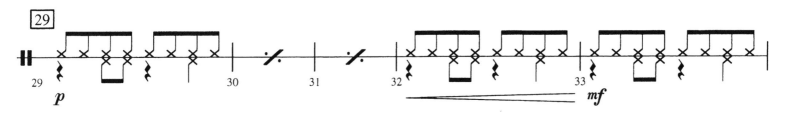

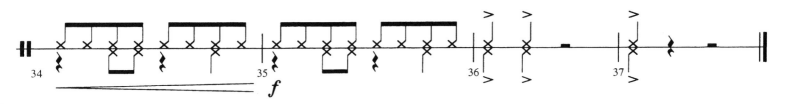

00860176

ROYAL FIREWORKS MUSIC

PERCUSSION 1
Snare Drum, Bass Drum

GEORGE FREDERIC HANDEL
Arranged by MICHAEL SWEENEY

00860176

ROYAL FIREWORKS MUSIC

George Frederic Handel
Arranged by MICHAEL SWEENEY

PERCUSSION 2
Cr. Cym.

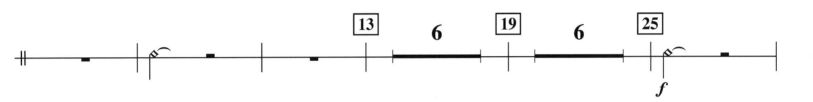

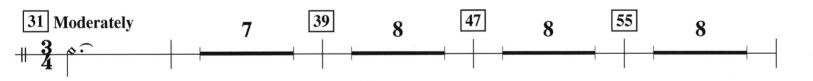

00860176

SCARBOROUGH FAIR

PERCUSSION 1
Sus. Cym., Wind Chimes, B.D., S.D., Tri.

Traditional English
Arranged by JOHN MOSS

00860176

SCARBOROUGH FAIR

PERCUSSION 2
Sus. Cym.

Traditional English
Arranged by JOHN MOSS

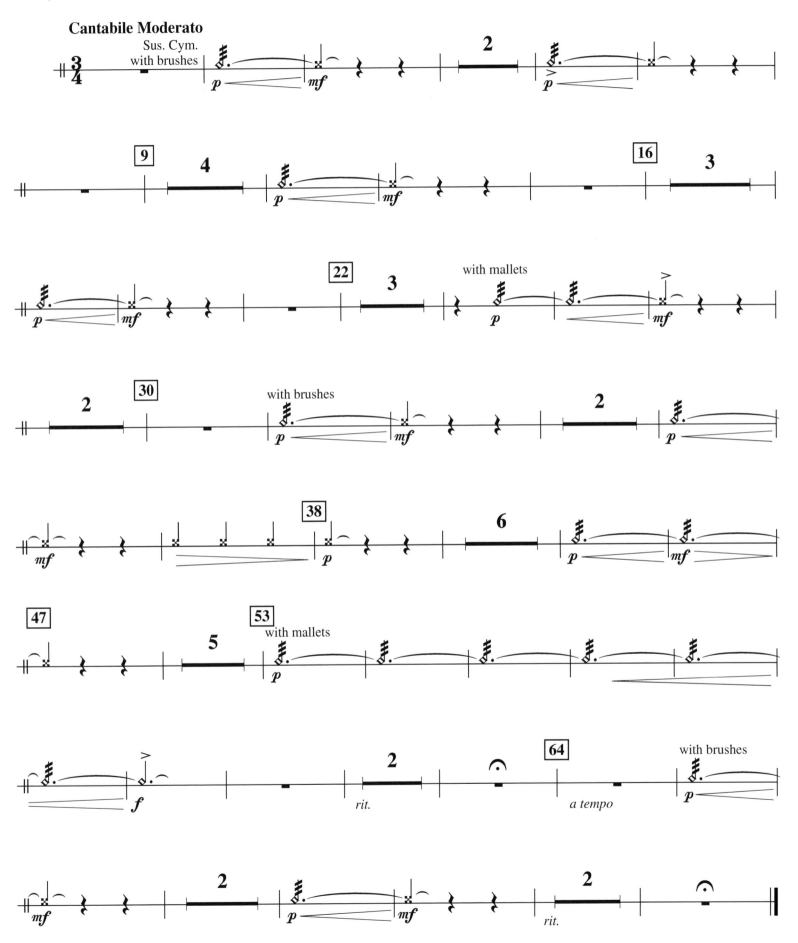